To Jen

Thanks for all you do!

Lar

After more than a decade of working with thousands of singles from Seattle to Miami and being instrumental in more than fifty marriages, I have compiled this book of basic dating dos and don'ts. I have seen so many crazy mistakes made by good people. It's time for a change. So for all you singletons out there who find yourselves flailing in the shitty, black hole of dating hell, it's time for you to master the dating world! Now is the time to take action, get out there, and find your golden goose!

—Kara Donahue

intheloopsingles.com

The Golden Goose

The Ultimate Guide to Dating in Your Lane

The Golden Goose
The Ultimate Guide to Dating in Your Lane

Kara Donahue

Contents:

ISBN: 198143125X
ISBN-13: 9781981431250

Acknowledgments

Thanks to my amazing staff at In the Loop Singles. They make me laugh daily and have endured me talking about this book for way too long. To the scores of singles who have been the inspiration for this book, allowed me to interview them (bug them), and have been some of the best friends of my life, I thank you. To my family, who supports me and whose encouragement has meant the world to me, I appreciate you. Oh, and sorry for the foul language and penis talk, Mom.

Preface

Golden Goose (gōldən gōos/)

A girl/guy everyone calls *hot* as hell, yet no one has ever gotten with her or him; therefore, the ultimate catch—a golden goose.

Example: "No, bro, you say you hit that, but no one has ever hit that. She's just a golden goose."

Golden Gooser ('gōldən gōoser/)

Someone who wants a mate who is better looking, more educated, more charismatic, sexier, funnier, smarter, more desirable, more financially stable, more interesting, more fit...basically someone who is completely out of his or her league. Golden goosers are typically PAF (Picky as Fuck) with absolutely no right to be so and have no self-awareness whatsoever.

Dating Sucks

Dating sucks—really, really sucks. Why can't we just get past the bogus online profiles to the contrived texting to the sexting to the date planning to the actual meeting (if it ever happens) to the letdown *or* the one-night stand (*letdown*) to the next suitor? Really? God! Wouldn't it be nice to just *find your person* without the agony and second-guessing, the time and energy, *and* the disappointment? To just be done with it?

Here I am. Here you are. We are equally attractive or almost equally attractive. We both like sushi and skiing. We hate old movies and bad drivers. We are on the same socioeconomic level. Our education is about the same. We have some great inside jokes. We have some mutual friends. You like blow jobs. I don't mind giving them. I like expensive shoes. You don't mind buying them. We want to live in the same area. I can tolerate your family we never see. You can tolerate my family we *always* see. I like to spoon. You will spoon. I don't try to change you (except your clothes, your hair, and the friends I hate of yours, whom we will not see). I stay in the same fifteen-pound range of when we met and will fuck you somewhat regularly. You support me. I support you. You listen to me, give me attention, and accept me. We like kissing each other. I don't nag that much. We are faithful to each other. We both want two kids and *done!* Voilà.

Your Person

But it never happens that way. It's exhausting. The reason is dating is *not* the same as it was before. Male and female roles are not the same as they were before (*before* as in the last generation-ish).

Think about this. According to my mom, who was born in 1951, guys would ask for your number, call you up, ask you out on a date that *they* planned, pick you up, take you to dinner or whatever, and *pay*, and you did not have sex with them. And they would actually ask you out *again*. They would court you. Whhhat? Not even a handy, Mom? Nope. Not even a kiss? A kiss, yes. But *people dated*.

Let's fast-forward to me. I was born in 1974. I hear that in the late eighties and early nineties, when I was in high school, people would still go out on dates. The getting of the number was still happening. The phone calls, the conversations, the movies, the dinners...Did the guy have a better chance of getting laid in 1991 than in 1967? *Yes*, but it wasn't a given.

By the way, I "*heard*" this because in high school I was 260 pounds with a bleached-blond afro and a loud, shitty attitude, and I was a big musical theater fan with a posse of gay friends. This was well before *Glee*, so I hear that dating was like this in the early nineties. I saw my friends do this, but I was singing songs from *Les Mis* with my pack of fat, dorky, mega-weirdo friends and not getting laid or dating at all. Regardless. *People dated.* They talked face-to-face and got to know one another. They had real relationships. They had real friends. They didn't text and surf the net while at dinner with people. They communicated the old-fashioned way. They talked.

With the Internet, right now, *everything* is at your fingertips. You want to see which dudes in a certain age range who live in a five-mile radius of you are single and ready to mingle? Swipe to the left. You want to see a parade of single chicks in a certain age range and the best picture of themselves they have ever taken and a bio of bullshit for you to judge- join Plenty of Fish for free! Just know you may be spending a ton of energy trying to figure out who is *really* single? Who is really HWP? And who is really not a weirdo in Pakistan trying to get your credit card info. It's hard, and it's not *natural*.

The Internet is here to stay. Apps are here to stay. Dating is almost dead. Hooking up is the norm.

A quick in and out and then off to greener pastures. That is not going to change. It's probably going to get worse. I am not writing this because I think this little book is going to make that much of a difference in how people interact with one another on the Internet. People aren't all of a sudden going to go back to 1955 and court and date and blah, blah, blah. For so many sociological reasons— women's lib, the sexual revolution, Photoshop, porn—that's not going to happen. We have lost the ability to build real, solid relationships. We don't date. We judge and move on. Therefore, so many people are alone or more isolated than ever—even though we still crave companionship, even though most people want *their person*.

I'm a realist.

However, there are some singletons who sincerely want to meet their persons, who want to have someone to hold hands with and smooch and eat food and laugh with, who truly want to share and build their lives with someone.

If that is *you*, read this. Here are my strategies. They work.

Chapter 1
Cast a Wide Net; It's a Numbers Game

After meeting and coaching more than ten thousand singles in the last ten-plus years, I've seen a lot of dating strategies that have bombed. To meet someone, you will have to do something radical. You will have to *try*. You will have to make it a priority. We work our asses off to finish school, get a good job, buy a house, and so on; we don't think these things should fall in our laps. But somehow, we do think relationships should fall magically from the sky. They usually don't.

My suggestion is this. Put your eggs in a ton of baskets. Try out several avenues of meeting new people and see what's working. If you want something, go after it. It's *not* desperate. It's proactive. This is going to take time. This is going to be a little part-time job for you. Here are some avenues you need to explore. Remember, it's a *numbers* game.

Here are some baskets to put your eggs in:

Join an *activities and travel club* for singles, like mine, In the Loop Singles. It's easy and comfortable to meet new people while you are doing something fun like enjoying a wine tasting or an all-day hike. Meeting people face-to-face is *key* in making a real connection. Getting out of the house is always a positive. It's a win-win.

Investigate at least five *online dating sites*. I highly recommend a paid site. Free sites like Plenty of Fish are usually packed with weirdos, desperados, people just scraping by with MWJs (minimum-wage jobs), and scammers. If they have a problem paying thirty-five bucks a month to meet singles, you can look forward to Taco Bell and no medical insurance. Read reviews and pick your top two. Don't splatter yourself on every single site. Farmers Only may not be your cup of tea. Pick two. (We will go over your profile in chapter 2.)

Think outside the box when considering meeting someone you usually wouldn't go for online. You may be a five-foot-ten-inch woman, and he's a five-foot-eight-inch man—not your usual suitor. But you never know. He could be hilarious and a beast in bed. Open up your criteria and be open-minded about chatting with someone new. We will address this at length in chapter 4, Know Your Fucking Lane.

Explore Dating Apps. Dating apps are here to stay. Tinder and Bumble are really popular right now. When this book is finally published, I'm sure ten more apps will be trending. That being said, from what I have seen, the majority of people using these apps are looking for a hookup verses a relationship. If that's your goal, sign up! The apps are fun and entertaining. Judging others while sitting on the toilet at your house is a guilty pleasure for many. But it's a lot of energy without a big return. I suggest only trying it out for two weeks. If it doesn't bare any fruit, delete. Also, just a heads-up, be aware that lots and lots of people are on this app, and the valet you just left your car with swiped past you ten minutes ago.

Be a joiner! Join an adult kickball team. Take golf lessons. Join the local chamber of commerce. Look into a young professionals' club or your college's alumni club. There are so many activities and groups out there to be a part of. Keep in mind that if you are a woman and you join a knitting club, *no guys* will be there. No guys are crocheting booties on the weekend. Also, for the men out there, join a spin class or a wine-tasting club, but don't sign up for a pole-dancing class. Don't sign up for a belly dancing course. You will be the Creepy Creeperson in the corner, trying to camouflage your boner. The women will not think it's cute that you are participating. You will be a pariah.

Hit up your *friends and family*! You may have a friend who works with a gorgeous and interesting woman. Your brother's best friend may be the bomb. Do not be afraid to ask for an introduction. It doesn't have to be a setup date. In fact, I recommend that it's not a date. Think more along the lines of meeting everyone while they are at a happy hour. Go to your cousin's wedding and talk to new people. Go to your neighbors' Fourth of July party, and get ready to socialize. Your friends and family may need a nudge in the right direction, especially if they are married. When people get married, their singles radar is out of commission. Express to them your desire to meet someone and tell them to rack their brains for some singles you haven't met yet, that they know.

Approach matchmaking and dating services with caution. Thumbs-up or thumbs-down on matchmakers and dating services really depends on who the matcher is. Being in the business and running activities clubs for singles for more than ten years has given me the opportunity to meet lots of matchmakers and people who work in the dating-service industry. For the most part, these folks are odd, narcissistic, used-car-salesman types; bullshitters with little to offer people; and mostly gigantic assholes. This is *not* all of them. A few (very few) are good, kind people who have a gift for bringing people together.

If you are looking into working with a matchmaker, there are a few things you need to ask before you sign up for the service:

1. How many people do they have in their rolodex right now who suit your criteria for a mate?

2. What is their screening process?

3. How do they recruit new singles?

4. Do they have profile pictures of current members?

5. Do they charge the same for men as they do for women?

6. What are they guaranteeing?

By the way, you should never accept the first price they offer you for their service. *Negotiate.* Ask to chat with some current singles they are working with. Be ready to throw down between $3,000 and $6,000 or more. Also, read online reviews thoughtfully. Some reviews are from sad, pathetic assholes whom nobody would ever want to date. Some are from real, normal people who have had good or bad experiences. Also, people are more apt to write a crappy review on Yelp than a good one. That's what Yelp is all about—letting people bitch publicly, letting bored dicks air their innermost thoughts.

Be visible. Put down the mouse and get out of your house. You need to be visible. That means go do some busywork at a Starbucks, not at your home office. Go watch the game at a hip bar, not on your couch. Start familiarizing yourself with the nightlife in your area. Know which bars and hotspots are popular with your age group. Use Google and ask around. While you're at a bar, ask the bartender which night is the most popular. Maybe it's Taco

Tuesday? Maybe it's Sunday's mimosa brunch? Find out, and then show up. Be *visible*. Go to things you enjoy. If you love to karaoke, do that. If you like playing pool, do that. Make this as fun for yourself as possible.

Be bold. You are going to have to get over being scared to talk to a stranger. If you are in line at Target and a nice-looking guy is standing behind you, say hi. What's the worst thing that can happen? He blows you off? Who cares? It's a *numbers* game. The *more* single people you meet, the more opportunity you have to meet *your person*. Staying at home doesn't do shit for you. Mr. Right doesn't know where you live. Ms. Right isn't going to appear on your doorstep. Be assertive. Do something.

Volunteer. There are so many worthy causes out there for you to participate in. Go feed the homeless or help out at a senior center or the humane society. Volunteer for the big fundraising gala coming up. Again, this is growing your network of *new* people. Also, it can really fill your soul bucket.

Small town? *Travel.* If you live in a small town, you may have to travel. You may have to drive forty miles to go to a bar out of the realm of everyone you went to high school with. Make a plan to go to a music festival, drive to that professional hockey game at the coliseum, or sign up for that speed-dating event two towns over. Travel. Also, you will have to spend more time screening profiles online.

Use dating sites *judiciously*—when you are surfing the online sites, don't spend your entire life drudging through them. But give yourself twenty minutes a day to check your inbox and see who's new and who looks interesting. Send a poke or whatever. Be swift and organized about it. If someone does not respond, *delete*. Move on. Don't get all dreamy over a picture or profile. On paper, people can look amazing and appear to have this incredible life, and then in person, they suck. Don't focus too much on their profiles and pictures. This is a means to an end. Meet in *person*.

Finally, *fill your calendar.* An example of a proactive month would look like this: spending twenty minutes a day on your online dating sites and apps, going to a happy hour once a week, joining your singles' activity club and participating in three events a month, going to your kickball practice once a week, saying hi to one stranger once a week, doing work at a local coffee shop once a week, exchanging e-mails with someone who is not the usual date you look for twice a month, and so on. This will quadruple the number of people you meet every month.

Remember, you need to *meet people*—lots of them. To make it easy, here are fifty-five places to meet singles:

55 Places to Meet Singles

1. In the Loop Activity and Travel Club for Singles

2. Coffee shops

3. Driving ranges

4. Happy hours

5. Wine tastings

6. CrossFit and other high-intensity fitness classes

7. Grocery stores

8. Gyms

9. Commuter trains/buses

10. Dog parks

11. Target

12. Networking events

13. Movie theaters

14. Hotel bars/restaurants

15. Sporting events

16. The DMV

17. Beaches/poolside

18. Professional sporting events

19. Alumni events

20. Trivia nights

21. Online dating sites

22. Group vacations

23. Holiday parties

24. Bar crawls

25. Cooking classes

26. Partner dancing classes

27. Street fairs

28. Ski resorts

29. Sailing clubs

30. Running clubs/events

31. Online business or social communities

32. Farmer's markets

33. Concerts

34. Open mic nights

35. Boozy brunches

36. Sports bars

37. Toastmasters

38. Industry meetings

39. Local talks/readings

40. Adult education classes

41. Volunteer organizations

42. Fund-raisers

43. Music and art festivals

44. Social media

45. Religious and spiritual gatherings

46. Weddings

47. School reunions

48. At work

49. School sports events

50. Coed sports leagues

51. Private clubs

52. University campuses

53. Public parks

54. House parties

55. Obstacle-course-type fitness events

Chapter 2
Your Hook (Online Dating Pics and Profiles)

Hook

Now, what's your hook? It's important that you put your best foot forward. Let's start with your pic. You need to be realistic. It has to look like you. Be honest. But look your best and accentuate the positive! Here are ten basic online picture profile suggestions:

1. Use good lighting and flattering shots.
2. Angle your shot so you look the best.
3. Have a minimum of four to five pictures—the more, the better.
4. Don't use "Zoolander selfies," aka duck faces and glamour shots.
5. Some pictures should *not* be alone. You want to appear to have friends and a life. And make sure your friends are cool with using them on your profile.
6. Be active doing something you love—skiing, wine tasting, whatever.

7. Include your family, but keep children's faces out of it.
8. Include your pets.
9. Don't take your own picture in the mirror.
10. Have at least one full-body shot. It doesn't have to be in a bikini. But full body.

Visuals

This is my best friend, Robbi. She's a beauty. However, notice in the first picture, she looks average. Not in her best outfit. Not a great angle. It looks like she is on her way to church. That can be a boner killer for some.

Notice picture two. She's pulled together. Hot. Great angle. Good hair day. And not trying too hard with her tits or ass hanging out. And *wow!* She has a friend, too.

Look #1   Look #2

It's weird, but guys prefer look number two. Non-Grandma attire. Men like formfitting clothing? What? How *weird*. Now, keep in mind, it's better not to look like a hoochie, but *do* show off your assets.

Here's the deal though. Your pic is your selling point, your *hook*. If you have great hair, focus on that. If you have awesome legs, make sure they are visible in the pic. If you are looking only for sex, a sexy bathroom selfie with your tits out may be attractive to many suitors but probably not a lifetime mate. Make sure what you are advertising is what you are selling.

If you are a rich guy or gal and take a picture of yourself sitting on your new Maserati with a fan of hundred-dollar bills, don't get pissed if you attract a bunch of gold diggers. It's what you are selling. Women, if you post a "look at my big tits in this bathing suit" pic, don't be mad if a dude wants a piece of ass after your first caramel macchiato. That's what you advertised. #dontbeadumbass.

Your *hook* is your great picture of yourself and some *key* words that describe you, your selling points, and your slogan.

Writing Your Profile Content

"Funny, professional, active, and driven smartass looking for a sushi partner and travel buddy."

This shows the person has a job and a sense of humor, likes to travel and exercise, and likes sushi. Figure out your own slogan that represents you. Keep it short and sweet. Try to be witty and to the point.

Describing yourself and presenting yourself is hard. It puts everyone in a vulnerable position. *You are being judged.* And that doesn't feel great. But remember, the more your profile highlights what's great and different about you, the better. Describing yourself and bragging are two different things. If you are a great painter, it's OK to state that. It's also OK to be self-deprecating, but *do not* put yourself down. Here are some ideas on how to make your profile a good one. Remember not to ramble. Keep it fun and to the point.

What's in your profile? Here is a checklist of online profile do's and don'ts.

1. *Do* use spell-check. For the love of God! Spell-check your shit! Also, have someone

proofread it. If you cannot capitalize correctly and you can't spell, ask for help. You look like a fucking joke, and it's embarrassing.

2. *Do* show your personality. Pick your top five personality traits and describe them briefly. Do highlight your best personality traits. If you are funny, try to convey that. If you are sarcastic, kind, a smartass, introverted, and so on, be real about it, and be sincere.

3. *Do* be honest about who you are—your physical characteristics, where you are at in life, your intentions, your wants...never lie. Ever. Don't lie about your height, age, or weight; you'll be found out soon enough. You don't have to say, "I am five-foot-five and 195 pounds." You can say "five-five and thick." Don't lie about being divorced. Don't lie about the job you have. Don't lie.

4. *Do* be expressive about your career or ambition. Ambition can be attractive. So is a *job*! You don't have to brag but mentioning your career and things you are passionate about is great. If you work at Taco Bell part time, it is what it is. That is not the same as

managing a Fortune 500 business. Say you work at a restaurant and leave it at that.

5. *Do* convey your lifestyle. Be honest about your financial situation. You don't have to give away all your dirty details about how much you make and how much you have in the bank but communicate your lifestyle.

6. *Don't* puke your life story on everyone. All of this can be done in a few paragraphs. Most people are just looking at your pictures anyhow.

7. Again, *do* keep it short. Don't write a novel about your life story—who did you wrong, what kind of cereal you like, what your deal breakers are, the last vacation you went on, how you caught your boyfriend in bed with your best friend. This is not a Dr. Phil session. Be precise. Your novella doesn't do you any good. Nobody cares. It's emotional, self-serving vomit.

8. *Do not* dismiss online dating. Remember you *are* online, dating. Ranking it down when you are in the thick of online dating makes you look like a dick.

9. *Do* state your intention. For example, you could say, "I am looking for a long-term relationship that may progress to marriage," or "I am looking for casual sex and a fun fuck buddy."

10. When describing what you're looking for in a partner, *don't* go negative. Listing four to five traits you really go for and a couple of deal breakers is important.

11. Never use your profile to write about the ex or whine. Taking a big steamer on your ex is *not* attractive, especially on an online profile.

12. Never divulge too much personal information. The dude looking at your profile could be Ted Bundy or some pathetic asswipe, and he doesn't need to know you work out at 24-Hour Fitness in Bellevue, Washington, every morning at 6:00 a.m. or that you work at Amazon in their Seattle office in suite 305. Stalkers and weirdos are everywhere. Be safe. No addresses, e-mails, nothing. A cell phone number maybe, but *nothing else*.

13. Maintain a 75/25 split between what you're like and what you want. I hate when people

write like three lines about themselves and then an encyclopedia about who they want. "Hi, my name is Becky. I work in human resources and live in Redmond, and I have two dogs. But I want a specific hair color, eye color, height, waist size, education level, fitness level, spirituality and religious affiliation, specific hobbies you participate in, political beliefs, food allergies, family connections, traveling preferences, what you eat for breakfast...I want to know specifically whether you wipe your butt front to back or back to front, where you shop, what car you drive...blah, blah, blah." People are visiting your profile to read about *you*, not what *you* think *they* should be.

14. *Don't* put yourself down. Being self-deprecating can be cute, but saying, "Man, I have a fat ass!" or "Dang, I have a tiny penis!" will not do you any good. Again, they will know soon enough.

15. *Don't* look like a giant pervert. Edit out your home dungeon or how great you are at eating vag. Again, they will find out. That's not for your profile. That info should be

divulged well into dating each other, over a bottle of pinot.

16. If you have to come up with a tagline, *do* try not to be corny. Look at a bunch of other people's taglines, find one that you think is cute, and do something like that.

Etiquette

Don't play games. If people are interested in you and you are not interested in them, be kind. Be really nice but be honest and tell them you are not interested. You are flattered and thank them for their interest. Don't *ghost* people. Be honest. If you are not interested, keep it short and sweet. If they react badly to that, block them.

If you *are* interested, return their call. Don't wait a month before getting back to someone. Make a plan to see them again and be open and honest.

Here is another revelation for some of you... If people are *not* responding to you, move on. *They are not interested.* Get a clue. They are not stuck under a bus. They have not recently been kidnapped. They are not pining for you, alone at home...worried you will not return their undying affections and therefore too scared to call you. They are simply *not* interested. You could be the bee's knees, and sometimes, they are *not* interested. Move on. This also applies to hitting on someone at a bar and constantly asking some coworker out. If the person says no, avoids getting together, or his or her body language says, "Fuck off," then please, fuck off. This is important.

Don't be a butthole about it either. Move on and leave the person alone. When you react poorly to ghosting or people not responding to you, it makes you look sad and even less attractive. This is not brain surgery folks.

Chapter 3

Deal Breakers

When looking for a mate, we all have a set of characteristics, *deal breakers*, that we cannot tolerate in the other person. As an exercise, please write down your top twelve deal breakers below. Really take some time and think about what is truly important to you.

For example, "smoker" may be a deal breaker. It could be a certain education level. A certain religion may be a deal breaker. Maybe you don't want to hump a racist? Maybe you don't want to blow a Klan member? Maybe you would rather not receive a rim job from a weekend karaoke host. Maybe you don't want to sit on the Unabomber's face... I don't know. It could be a certain height you prefer...you pick.

1.
2.
3.
4.
5.

6.

7.

8.

9.

10.

11.

12.

Now that you've finished, the next step is to circle the top five deal breakers you wrote down and discard the rest. Yep! Five deal breakers is quite enough. No need to be PAF (*Picky as Fuck*). Really. Every single person out there who is looking for a mate needs to keep his or her deal breakers down to five. Also, if more than two of your top five deal breakers are about someone's appearance, you need to put yourself in check. You are shallow and need to think about priorities. Tall and fit is enough. Tall, fit, tan, wavy hair, and green eyes is *too much*.

Deal breakers are important. We all have things in someone else we cannot live with. It's good to have standards. But when your laundry list for a suitable mate reads like *War and Peace*, you have some self-reflection work to do.

Deal breakers are just a start. The three most important things that keep a relationship together are you two *having the same value system, both being dedicated to making this relationship work,* and *going in the same direction.*

Values Example

I went out with a really fantastic, attractive guy for about six months several years ago. He grew up Bible-Belt Baptist and super right-wing. I, in contrast, grew up in a liberal Pacific Northwest family who never attended church. After the passion faded a bit in our relationship, we realized our core values were so different that our relationship would not work.

Dedication Example

If he is totally ready to go the whole way with you, the marathon, through thick and thin, and you aren't willing to do that for him, address this. You might be a slow simmer. See how everything shakes out and *then* let him go if your feelings don't change.

Direction Example

If you have a great job, maybe are in school getting your master's, have your 401(k), and are working hard for a successful, financially stable life, yet you are dating a person who maybe wants to buy a Winnebago and travel the United States living off the land, it ain't gonna work. Talk about where you see yourself in five years, ten years, and so on. If your partner wants to move to Hawaii and you want to stay in San Francisco, that's a problem. You want kids, and he or she doesn't? Problem.

Ask questions. Don't compromise on the really important deal breakers. But to be more successful at dating and meeting people, you have to loosen up on the deal breakers that are meaningless. If hair color is a deal breaker, then you have some soul-searching to do. If a specific profession is what you are looking for, you have some more soul-searching to do. Having standards is one thing; being ridiculous about deal breakers will guarantee you remain alone, watching your friends enjoy their happy lives.

Research

After interviewing one hundred male singles and one hundred female singles between the ages of twenty-one and sixty-five of all backgrounds in the Seattle area, the following deal breakers were the most important to men and women.

Top Five Deal breakers for Men: What They Do Not Want in Their Ladies

1. Overweight

2. Not sexual

3. Dishonest

4. High maintenance

5. Clingy

Top Five Deal Breakers for Women: What They Do Not Want in Their Men

1. No job

2. Liars

3. Short stature

4. Cheaters

5. Bad hygiene

Of course, there are exceptions to these rules. Maybe if we interviewed two thousand singles, there would be different results, but here they are. After working with singles daily for more than ten years, none of the results surprised me in the least. So, let's talk truth.

Truth

If you are a woman looking over the results, you will see that weight is the number-one deal breaker for men. Even those men over sixty years of age who were surveyed preferred a height-weight proportionate (HWP) mate. This is frustrating. It sucks, frankly. I have seen women who are skinny and below-average looking with crappy personalities date constantly. Then I have seen *beautiful* plus-size women who are absolutely fantastic never date at all. There are so many things wrong about this. I hate it. But here's the truth.

If you are overweight, dating is way more difficult. There are exceptions to this rule, and I have met plenty of dudes who like some meat on the bone. I married one. But if you really want to meet someone special, do something about your fitness level, period. We all want to have someone love us just the way we are. Men are visual, ladies, so to open up a wider group of people to date, being height-weight proportionate is a big factor. I hate this. It's not fair, but you need to lose the weight. By the way, I am a chunk and *hate* writing this down, but it's something I see every day. I will say that in my dating life, when I have lost twenty pounds and am close to my goal weight, *way* more guys have asked me out. Male friends of mine have told me I was dating turds because of the extra weight I was carrying. Truth. Been there.

Men, the ladies have spoken. They care about your *job*. This also did not come as a surprise. Women want stability, and a low-income or minimum-wage job means we have to carry *you*. Women *hate* this. There is quite a bit of value placed on women's looks and quite a bit of value placed on a man's income level. Truth, men—pull your finances together. Hustle. You don't have to be a millionaire but work on being stable. A woman does not want to date some albatross who doesn't have two quarters to rub together. Hustle and drive are super attractive. So, if your income is not great, seeing that you are busting ass is a *good thing*. You also may have plenty of characteristics that women love, and your wallet may be of no consequence at all.

This brings me to the most important chapter. Y'all need to know *your dating lane*.

Chapter 4

Know Your Fucking Lane

I'm soooo over talking to people about who *they* want to find and the ridiculous checklists they have, especially those who have very little going on. OK, so you're broke, butt-ugly, one hundred pounds overweight with an oozing boil in the middle of your forehead, living in your mom's basement, and eating out of garbage cans, but you want to date a rich supermodel with a six-pack who runs a nonprofit organization and speaks eight languages. Stop it. You need to know your lane. *Know your fucking lane!* Please, for God's sake, let me help you!

Lane Quiz

Test #1: Fill this out. Give a rating from 1–10, 10 being the highest.

Identify the *lowest* number in each category you are OK with dating. For example, I am OK with dating a guy who's only a 6 in looks, but I like smart guys, so he would have to be an 8 in intelligence.

Jot down the number that coordinates with your preference for said mate:

Lane Quiz, Part 1

Them:
1. Looks: _____
2. Personality: _____
3. Personal success: _____
4. Intelligence: _____
5. Fitness level: _____
6. Emotional stability: _____
7. Integrity: _____
8. Confidence: _____
9. Spiritual commitment: _____
10. Skills in the sack: _____

One of the biggest issues in dating today is everyone wants a 10, a golden goose, if you will. A guy could be fifty-eight years old, five-two, three hundred pounds, missing his four front teeth, and working at Jiffy Lube, and he wants to date a Carrie Underwood lookalike who is twenty-nine and just won the Hawaiian Tropics Global Bikini Contest. Seriously. Oh, and it's not just guys who are living in Oz. I have been working and meeting with singles daily for more than ten years, and I would say at least 85 percent of these singles want a mate who has more going on for them than they do. Maybe it's a delusion. Maybe it's the media. Maybe it's the never-ending access to other singles—the grass-is-always-greener mentality. Maybe it's that people don't have a realistic view of how they are perceived by others and what's *really in their lane.* But this is an epidemic. This is why soooo many people are single and lonely. A guy from work who is nice, and fun asks you out, but you don't go out with him because he is fifteen pounds overweight or doesn't own his own home? Stupid.

Maybe there is a woman at the gym who is friendly, great to talk with, and fairly attractive, but you don't go out with her because you are holding out for a stone-cold ten to impress your friends? Stupid.

One of the things that will help you be more successful in dating is knowing your lane and staying in your lane.

Your Lane

There are always exceptions to your lane. I could write a chapter about the exceptions to this rule. Look at Donald Trump. He is a fat, ugly asshole who is rich, and Melania is gorgeous, about twenty-five years younger than Donald, and appears to be intelligent. How did that match happen? Hmmm, I wonder?

Generally speaking, if you stay in your lane, you will have more success in meeting someone who is right for you, meeting *your person*.
How do you determine what your lane is and who you should be focusing on? Here's my quiz.

Lane Quiz, Part 2

While taking this quiz, you must be brutally honest with yourself. Here's how it works: There are ten lanes you will be evaluating for yourself. How you evaluate your number in any given lane is based upon your social circle.

For example, if I were to base my looks rating against Jennifer Aniston's looks, with Jennifer being a 10, I would be a 4. But instead, I am basing my looks level in comparison to those people I interact with, or my social circle. For example, my rating would be based on the hottest chick I work with or the most beautiful daughter of my mom's best friend. If she is a 10, then maybe I am a 7. If I were basing my success level against Bill Gates's success level, him being a 10, I would be a 1, or a 0. But I am basing my success lane on the people I personally know and interact with in my social circle. So therefore, I would be more like an 8, if comparing myself to the most successful person I personally know.

Also, as a side note, just because you played varsity football in high school twenty years ago does not mean you are still athletic. Be realistic with these ratings!

Your Lane Quiz: Fill this out. Give a rating from 1–10, 10 being the highest.

1. Looks: _____
2. Personality: _____
3. Personal success: _____
4. Intelligence: _____
5. Fitness level: _____
6. Emotional stability: _____
7. Integrity: _____
8. Confidence: _____
9. Spiritual commitment: _____
10. Skills in the sack: _____

1) Now, drop all of your numbers by 1 point. The top three are your strongest traits. This is your lane, your triad. Write them down here.

_____, _____, and

_____

2) Know your triad. These characteristics should be close to what you should be focusing on in finding your significant other. So, for example, your top numbers may look like this: 8 in personality, 8 in success, 9 in integrity, 7 in looks.

Your Triad: Personality, Success, Integrity

Example:

So, you would look for a successful person with a great personality who is sincere and easy on the eyes. There is wiggle room with this of course. Just be aware of where you are at.

Next, take a look at your ideal mate's ratings that you filled out earlier. Are there some discrepancies between those numbers and yours? When dating someone, it will behoove you to stay within a point of where you are in the given categories. For example, if you are a 5 on fitness level, don't expect to date a 10 on the fitness scale. If you are a 9 in emotional stability, you won't be happy dating a 2 (aka a hot mess) on the emotional stability scale.

Here's a bit more assistance in this.

I'm a personality 9, skills in sack 8, and confidence 8. I should go for guys who have a witty personality, are self-assured, and can keep up in the sex department.

Just because I am a 6–7 in looks and it's not in my triad doesn't mean that I have to bang Quasimodo. It just means that my top four should be in line with my person's triad.

Mind the Gaps!

I am beating this like a dead horse, but really look at your person's ratings and yours. If there are some big gaps in these numbers, you need to put yourself in check. You may be a *golden gooser*, wanting the golden goose, despite where you are truly at. This is a great recipe for being alone for the rest of your life. You can twiddle your thumbs at home, alone, watching Netflix as all your friends get married and have kids. You can masturbate to Pornhub on your phone instead of having a real relationship, because you are holding out for a young, gorgeous Channing Tatum look-alike. You may have a forty-inch waist but refuse to date a "fat girl." You make $28,000 a year but want to date a millionaire. The list goes on. Stay in your *lane*! For God's sake, stay in your fucking *lane*! Think about this. Be honest with yourself. You will be happier and more successful with your dating.

On the flip side, if your numbers are a lot higher than what you expect from a mate, raise your standards a bit. It's OK to want someone who has as much to offer as you do. Don't settle for an army of turd burgers. If *you* bring something great to the table, so should they!

It's important that you have your most *honest* (not nicest) friend double-check your ratings. Ask them what your triad is to verify the real deal.

Know that your triad is not set in stone either. You can change lanes. People do it all the time. Here are some strategies to boost your rating.

Chapter 5
Give Yourself a Boost!

How to Boost Your Rating

1. Looks

Men, go to the men's department at a nice store like a Nordstrom. Ask a decent-looking woman who works there to help you with some basics: a good pair of jeans, a nice pair of khakis or dress-up pants, a couple of button-up shirts, a nice pair of shoes, and a few casual shirts. If you're fifty-five, don't try to dress like you are twenty, but keep it a bit *younger*. This is going to cost about $500 to $600, minimum. Don't buy your clothes at Costco or at a garage sale or something. Don't be cheap. You don't have to do a whole new wardrobe, but get a couple of decent pieces. Also, if you wear glasses, get some hip glasses. Even if you are ninety, get some good-looking glasses. Also, spend some money on a good haircut, and make sure your teeth don't look shitty.

Women, men are visual. They enjoy tits and ass. Be yourself, but dress with a teeny bit of sex appeal, not like you are going to your grandma's bingo night. Get your hair and makeup done at a nice, professional place. Spend some money. Go to a good salon and have them help you. Don't try to foil your hair at home or give yourself a fucking haircut. Wear clothes that accentuate your body type. Dress for your age but hip and fashion forward. Always pull it together. Don't go to Safeway in a pair of dirty sweats with no bra on and your hair in a scrunchie...Mr. Right may be at Safeway buying a rib eye, and you look like a Turd Ferg in your Lane Bryant sweatpants. Always pull it together.

2. Personality

If you have a shitty personality, you probably aren't aware that you suck. Most people with shitty personalities are clueless. But here are some helpful tips if you have a hard time interacting with others and keeping friends.

- Be curious. Ask people questions about their lives.

- Don't be judgey and snoopy.

- Relax.

- Try to smile and be friendly.

- Talk to people about your interests.

- Find common ground with people.

- Get a hobby or two so your life isn't so boring and you have something to discuss with others.

- Avoid religion and politics when first getting to know people.

- Avoid asking about someone's exes and telling horror stories about yours.

- Open up.

- Be interested in others.

3. Personal Success

This looks different for everyone. But *hustle* is sexy. Upward mobility is sexy. Taking care of business is sexy. Moochers and sad saps who are looking for a handout or constantly in need of help are boner killers.
- Be motivated.

- Work hard.
- Get a better job; try harder.

4. Intelligence

Stay aware of what's going on around you. I mean, really, intelligence is not something you can necessarily control, but being informed and well-read *is* something you can control.
- Read more.
- Be more informed.

5. Fitness Level

If you prefer someone who is in good shape, you need to be in good shape yourself. There are gyms, personal trainers, and weight-management businesses available. Seek them out. You have control over a fat ass.

6. Emotional Stability

If you have some emotional problems, it's OK. Lots of people do. Most, I think. See someone about this. Seek help. You can change this. Try not to drag old baggage into new relationships. But take care of yourself. The more you like yourself, the easier relationships become. Stop expecting others to fill a void or save you. You gotta fill your own bucket. Don't be afraid to get that part of your life square. Everyone has his or her own shit going on; you are not alone in this. Therapy is good. Sad and depressed is bad.

7. Integrity

This is usually a serious value system issue. This is not quick fix. But to take a step in the right direction, be honest. Don't make any promises you can't keep. Don't blow people off. Be kind. Be straightforward. If you have had a problem being a cheater or your follow-through has been crappy, take actions to change this. You can improve. Liars spread misery. Step up and be a solid, good human. Don't lie.

8. Confidence

Ultimately, you have to feel good about yourself. Try not to be consumed by what other people think of you. I would much rather be with an average-looking guy who carries himself with confidence than a gorgeous man who is insecure. Confidence is *attractive*. It's magnetic. If you are lacking in this department, fake it till you make it. Project confidence, and you'll attract more confident people. Do things that make you feel more confident. Dress the part. Be bold. Try. Google this. There are a million articles online specifically about this very topic.

9. Spiritual commitment

If you expect that of your mate, then walk the walk yourself. This is a huge deal breaker for most. Be true to this.

10. Good in the sack

Ummmmm, practice (safe practice makes perfect). Watch some porn, get some new ideas, ask your partner what he or she likes, communicate, and be confident. If perhaps you have a tiny penis, you may have to really learn how to eat pussy. If you are a chick who is a lights-off-missionary-only-humps-once-a-month-no-dick-suck kind of gal- good luck with that. Sex is important.

Ultimately, you are in charge of *you*. You are in charge of *your lane*. Wanting someone with more to offer than you do doesn't bode well in the dating realm. Making changes is not easy, but it can be done.

Chapter 6

Red Flags

When you are looking to date someone, there are some basic characteristics or actions you need to avoid. These are *red flags*.

Red-Flag Checklist: Forty-Six Basic Red Flags

1. The person has three friends on Facebook. (This person is trying to recruit you for ISIS.)
2. The person has no real-life friends.
3. He or she obviously has a significant other on social media.
4. He or she won't give you a last name.
5. He or she won't speak with you—only texts and e-mails. (Get the person on the phone within two days of communication. You can tell if someone sucks within five minutes on the phone.)
6. He or she won't meet you face-to-face within *one* week. The person may be in prison, married, full of shit, or playing games.
7. The person lives in another country. Unless you met on a cruise and fell in love or

something, don't waste time on people who live far away.

8. He or she says inflammatory things, such as "I hate gays," "Kill the Jews," or "Women aren't as smart as men." If the person is offending you from the beginning, it will only get worse. *Move on.* These are assholes.

9. He or she has a MWJ (minimum-wage job). If *you* have an MWJ and he or she has an MWJ, that's fine. Maybe if the person has an MWJ but is putting him- or herself through school, it's OK. The person is a work in progress. If you are in a great financial situation and the person seems fun and wonderful and you don't care about finances, perhaps an MWJ is OK. Other than that, it's *not OK.*

10. He or she is a LIB (*live with parents* aka, "Live In Basement"). If you live with your parents, it's OK. If the person's mom or dad is dying of cancer, and he or she is saving the day, it's OK. Every other LIB is *not* OK.

11. Living with an ex is not OK—*ever.*

12. The person has more than four cats.

13. The person owns birds. If *you* own birds, marry them.

14. He or she is on the phone and online too much.
15. His or her personal hygiene is gross. The person is dirty. Everyone pretty much has the ability to shower. The person can go to a fucking McDonald's and use their soap and paper towels and wipe that ass up. If the person just ran the Marathon for Hope or something, possibly OK. But he or she should be respectful enough to clean up when you meet.
16. He or she hates his or her family or has no contact with them. There are exceptions, but generally, this is not a good sign.
17. All the person's exes are "crazy." If he or she has one or two exes who are crazy, shit happens. If they *are all crazy,* it's actually your potential partner who sucks.
18. He or she has no transportation. If you live in New York City or some walkable town, it's OK, of course. But if you live in Wichita and have no car, that's a problem. Dig into this a bit; there could be explanations.
19. He or she doesn't return phone calls or texts.

20. He or she texts too much. (Too much is completely based on your perspective, by the way.)
21. He or she calls too much (same as above).
22. He or she swings by your place of work without asking.
23. He or she won't use protection. If the person is fucking you without a condom, he or she is fucking *everyone* without a condom, and you will have herpes within a month.
24. The person sends an unsolicited dick, boob, or vag porno pic before you *meet*.
25. He or she wants to just hook up and have sex—*unless* that is your motivation too. Then go for it! Otherwise, it's a *red flag*.
26. He or she lies about him- or herself when you meet in person. Move on.
27. He or she has too much contact with family. If the person goes to Mommy's house every day, it's weird. A close relationship with family is awesome. Hanging from the teat is not.
28. He or she has massive numbers of selfies on social media, including duck face and other sucky, self-serving selfies.

29. The person has bad grammar. This should be a given, but we fall in love with a fake profile so much and love the attention the person gives so much that we don't think about sentences like "I no go to work today," "You like restraint food?" "You want meet on Wedday?" or "Wanna make baby?" What the fuck? Also, side note, if the person can't spell-check on a basic level, he or she is lazy as fuck (LAF) and may be just short of getting a GED. And that means a minimum-wage job. You'll be footing the bill in the future and paying child support, so universally, stay away from bad grammar.

30. While dating, he or she takes his or her phone to the bathroom. Hmmm...secretive much? Also, *no one* should be on the phone while sitting on a public toilet. Or peeing in a urinal. Seriously.

31. The person does not follow through.

32. He or she is mean to waitstaff, animals, old people, and kids.

33. He or she focuses all conversations on him- or herself.

34. He or she puts you down.

35. The person can't keep a job.
36. He or she doesn't have a bank account.
37. He or she doesn't support his or her kids. Gross. Walk away from that bullshit. Talk about shitty integrity.
38. He or she always expects you to pay.
39. He or she is a hoarder.
40. He or she has been married and divorced more than three times. This is not a deal breaker but should give you pause.
41. He or she has multiple baby mommas or baby daddies and baby dramas.
42. He or she ghosts you. This means the person falls off the face of the earth, and you never hear from him or her again for *no* reason.
43. **Is lit all the time. *Drug and alcohol problems*.**
44. **Has mental issues.**
45. **Is abusive. IN ANY WAY.**
46. **Fucks other people.**

Red flags are important and need to be taken seriously. Again, go with your gut. If something feels off, it is. Don't waste your time. *Next*!

Chapter 7

Be a Good Date

Dating is a fine art, a skill. Most singletons are shitty at dating. So here are some basic tips you need to follow to be a good date. One thing in particular you need to do is give people a chance. If the person asking you out is not the usual type you go for, who cares? Go out with him or her anyhow, even just for coffee—you never know. If you are tall and love dating tall guys and he's an inch shorter than you, go out anyway. He may be hilarious and be packing nine inches. Who knows? Date outside the box a bit.

The Basics

1. Ask someone out clearly.

Don't just say or text, "Wanna hang out?" "Wanna hook up?" or "Wanna watch a movie on my couch?" Ask for a *real date*. Then make a plan. Ask your date what he or she likes. If you are the person asking someone out, you should have a plan for your date. If the plan is dinner and a comedy club, make reservations at a restaurant and buy tickets to the show. If the plan is to go

Rollerblading, then pick a day and have a plan for lunch or something afterward. You pay. Again, *you pay*. What that means is whoever asks for the date should *pay* for the date. If it's kind of a mutual, let's get together, the man should pay. I know that's not very progressive. But...still.

Now, don't go to the movies for a first date. Don't plan something where you two can't talk and get to know each other. Be creative. Google "Things to do in [your city]," and lots of ideas will pop up. Go to Groupon and see what's out there.

Making an effort makes the other person feel special, and that's a great way to start.

Don't go overboard and buy someone diamond earrings, and also make sure the date is no more than three to four hours. You don't want an all-day excursion until you know the person better. If it naturally leads to that, then great.

Don't suggest a dinner and movie night at your house, unless you are only looking for sex. We all know "Let's watch a movie at my place" means "I would like a blow job and piece of ass later at my house."

2. Show up and be on time.

Of course, show up. Never stand anyone up. Everyone is busy. Nobody has time to be stood up.

Be a decent human and be respectful. If you aren't going to go through with the date, you can call or text someone and be nice. Be on time. When you are late, you are telling the person your time is more important than his or hers.

3. Try to look good.

Pull it together. Show some effort. Always *look your best*. Looking shitty is for people in solid, monogamous relationships.

4. Put down your phone.

It's so Goddamn rude when you are constantly looking at your phone over dinner. Stop the madness and put it down for a friggin' hour.

Making Conversation

People like talking about themselves. So be curious on your date. If small talk is hard for you, memorize the following questions and use them for talking points. Don't *bombard* the person with these questions. Sprinkle them throughout the date. Build your dating skills. If making small talk is an issue for you, preparing a handful of questions will do you well.

Get-to-Know-Ya Questions

Memorize these—please, for the love of God.
1. Where did you grow up?
2. Tell me about your job.
3. How many siblings do you have?
4. What do your parents do for work?
5. Where did you go to school?
6. What do you like to do for fun?
7. Where do you love to travel?
8. What was your childhood like?
9. How do you like your job?
10. What kind of sports or activities do you like?
11. What's the earliest memory you have?
12. Where's the best place you ever went with your parents, and what did you do there?
13. Tell me about your best friend.
14. What kind of books (TV shows/movies/video games) do you like? Why?
15. What's the worst job you've ever had?
16. What did you enjoy (or hate) about school?

17. What's the most embarrassing moment of your life?

These questions are designed to spark some chatter. There aren't really any right or wrong answers; again, the way a person answers these questions can tell you more about him or her than the answers themselves.

Topics to Avoid on Your First Few Dates

Don't talk about the following:

1. Religion

2. Politics

3. Your ex

4. Personal problems

5. Family drama

6. Horrible child-custody issues

7. Your lower-back pain, wart on your penis, unidentifiable butt rash or any physical ailments

8. How much you hate your job

9. Your lack of funds

10. How horny you are

11. Mary Kay or Amway

Be fun. Have energy. Go with the flow. If it's a restaurant you have not heard of, just go. If it's not an activity you have tried before, be adventurous and just try it.

Women, this is for *you* to hear. If you are really looking for a long-term relationship, don't have sex on the first date. All the guys I talk to consistently say a woman's a ho if they get in her pants on the first date. Instead of the typical third-date rule, I suggest you only sleep with someone when you two are exclusive. He's only sleeping with you, and you are only sleeping with him.

For everyone, ask about your partner's sexual health and get checked out. You may not know you have a disease. He may not know if he has one. But be safe and smart about it.

Second-Date Etiquette

Ladies, if you only get one thing out of this chapter, it should be this: after the date, *do not text him or call him*. Do not reach out first. If he likes you, he will contact you. I repeat—do not reach out first. Ever. Period. Delete his number, so you can't reach out first. He can be a big boy and call or text you.

Men

Be a man, and call or text within two days. Don't play games. Be honest about your wants. The waiting of three days is exhausting and ridiculous. Let it go. You will still have your nut sack intact if you call the day after a great date.

You Are Not into the Person? That's Cool

If you aren't into the person, be honest. Don't flake out. It's not OK. Be truthful. Tell him or her, "Thanks for the date, but I don't see us being more than friends."

If the date was just so-so, give it another try. Some people are awful first daters. It's nerve-racking. The person could be having an off day. Give him or her another chance. If after the second date you're still not feeling it, *move on*.

Exclusive?

When should you ask if you are exclusive? This is different for everyone. I believe this all depends on when you become physical. But some people are OK with the person they are dating, dating others. It's a preference. But if you are looking for a long-term relationship with this person, I suggest you ask where you stand with him or her and ask if you are exclusive. If the person is seeing others and you don't like that, then break it off. You have a right to know. This is your health and your sanity. He or she may want to date around longer than you do. That's fine. But don't have sex with him or her if he or she is dating others. Go to the movies, hang out, and make out, but don't have sex.

You Can't Change Anyone

You can't change people. If someone says he or she does not want a serious relationship, there's nothing you can do to change his or her mind. If someone says he or she doesn't want kids, that person doesn't. If they don't want to get a better job, you can't make them get a better job. If they don't want to get into shape, you can't force them to get into shape.

These things are not challenges. You cannot change people. Listen to what they are telling you. Be cognizant of social cues and obvious signs. If he or she only calls you at 10:00 p.m. to come over, you are a booty call. If someone is reaching out to chat with you and shows you attention and consideration, that person is interested. Again, do not waste your time. *Your person* is out there waiting for you, so don't dick around with people who are not on the same page as you. While you are waiting around for Mr. /Ms. Wrong to get it together and be with you, Mr. /Ms. Right is passing you by.

Be respectful. If you decide to go to dinner with an online date person, finish the meal and be kind—unless the person is gross, awful, offensive, scary, or dishonest, you are in danger, or he or she is a certifiable weirdo. If so, beat it out of there and block him or her. But if the person simply isn't right for you, finish the meal and be polite. If the person comes in and is one hundred pounds more than his or her pic, you can still finish a meal and be a kind person. If the person is offensive, then, of course, leave. But don't just leave if you are not attracted to him or her. Sixty minutes out of your life will not kill you, and hurting people is just bad. Don't do it.

Suck it up. Be kind. You can certainly call someone out on a lie, but again, be nice.

Kissing

This is going to sound weird, but if you are unsure if you are a good kisser, you are going to have to fix that. How do you fix that? I suggest you find a friend, who is *just* a friend, who will be honest with you and make out with him or her. Get feedback and explain what you are doing. Yep, sounds weird, but it works. Also, practice on dates, even ones you aren't that into. Practice makes perfect. Also, men, go in for the kiss and take charge. Women, you can do the same thing.

Sex

This is such a personal thing. Never be afraid to ask who else people are fucking. If they are getting naked with you, you should be comfortable enough with them to find out what is going on. Before you have sex, I recommend *getting tested*. Be safe. Protect *yourself*. Be on the same page with your partner. Talk about it. Be a good communicator. Also have protection on you. Ladies, buy condoms.

If you don't know how you are in bed and are worried that you suck in the sack, practice with *everyone* you go on a date with! Everyone. Hump everyone!

Actually, you should watch some porn. See their techniques. See what looks hot and try to emulate that. Also, when you are with people, ask them what they like. Be a generous lover. Don't be crazy nervous; just simply ask. See what they are enjoying, and then do *more* of that.

Never do anything that makes you uncomfortable. And be as safe as possible at all times. Never pressure people to go further than they want.

If you are dating someone and think, "Tonight is the night," then wear good underwear and clean your place. Put on clean sheets and bring some freshening wipes with you. Nobody likes a dirty vag or cheesy penis. It's not that difficult to wipe your ass.

Conclusion

Dating is hard. It's going to take effort, time, and energy. Rarely will it fall in your lap. So, cast your net wide, and try dating people a bit outside your comfort zone. Be curious about others. Be honest and straightforward with your intentions. Don't be *too* needy. Stay in your lane. Don't hump everyone who buys you a cup of coffee. Guys, don't have sex with just anyone who is willing. Be choosy. Be good to others. Protect yourself from frauds and good-for-nothings. Flex your dating skills. Get what you want.

If you are dating more than one person at a time, be honest about it. You don't have to say, "Hey, I was sitting on Johnny's face ten minutes before our date." But you can certainly express that you are dating around right now.

When you find a good one, do not play hard to get. Be a good communicator. The whole wait three days before contacting them again is stupid. If you like someone, don't smother him or her but do stay in contact and make plans. If the person is a *keeper*, then know what you have and stop dating around. Stop it with the bologna and put yourself in it. Yes, we all have walls, but if you really want to be in a relationship, you have to be vulnerable and in it to win it.

Put these skills into action.

Chapter 8

Keeping It Goin'!

How do you keep this good relationship you just worked hard and drudged through weirdos and assholes to find?

Twenty Things You Can Do to Keep Your Relationship Going Strong

1. Make your partner your priority. No one wants to feel like second banana to your work, friends, kids, or social calendar.

2. Resolve arguments together. If you plan on being in this relationship forever, you better learn how to fight fair with your partner. It's hard to be adults and actually talk issues out and be willing to compromise. But *talk it out*, and don't be mean. Seek to see your partner's perspective.

3. Show affection daily—hugs, kisses, rubs, touching. This is *so* important. Make it a point every day to physically show love and *say* it. This also includes penetration. Your man *don't* just want a hug, OK?

4. Do the things you did the first year you were dating. Just because you are married doesn't mean the nice dinners, cute text messages, and blow jobs cease. Keep it up. Make an effort to show *effort* in your relationship. Look good and *try*.

5. Be an aficionado of your partner. You should know how he or she likes coffee, when to give him or her space, what activities he or she enjoys, and what makes him or her smile.

6. Have each other's back. Even when your partner is in the wrong, even when he or she pisses you off, have his or her back. You are his or her biggest supporter.

7. Ask for what you want. Guess what? Your person cannot read your mind. *Tell* him or her what you want. Don't suffer in silence and build up resentment. You can communicate this in a nice way. If you want more romantic dinners, ask. If you need more help around the house, ask. If you want to swing with the neighbors, simply ask.

8. Be brutally honest. This does not mean being awful and hurtful to your partner. It means you do not hide your feelings; let him or her know where you stand always.

9. Don't argue over money. You should know *well* before you are in the thick of it with this person how he or she manages money. Set the rules for money before you ever move in together. I suggest separate bank accounts and specific bill and responsibilities assigned to each person. You should discuss and monitor this, not fight about it.

10. Don't focus on little things that really don't matter. If she doesn't make the bed, if he tells crappy jokes, who cares? Let it go. If he's nasty to your kids, or if she's humping someone at work, then that's a different story.

11. Be yourself and take care of yourself: If you have to hide your quirkiness, if your partner hides his or her temper, at some point, this will *all* come out. Might as well be your weirdo selves from the get-go. Your relationship will eventually crumble if you don't. And self-care is

important. If you are happy, it only strengthens you as a couple.

12.   Create a weekly ritual to check-in with each other. This could be every Saturday morning you go to a local diner for breakfast together. Every Sunday night, it's *Game of Thrones* and margaritas. Rituals are *good*.

13.   Keep it sexy. Dirty sweatpants and thunderous farting in front of each other is not sexy. Sexiness is important. Romance is important. Buy the lingerie, book the oceanfront hotel, and squeeze in the fart. Make an effort to look good. Make an effort even when you "have a headache" to *do it*! If your partner isn't getting fed at home, he or she will go elsewhere for a sandwich. Don't leave him or her starving.

14.   Have lots of sex. I feel I have to state this a million times. So here it is again. Have sex a lot.

15.   Spend time apart. You are not connected at the hip. No couple spends every waking moment together. It's weird, and it ends up suffocating the other person. You have to have a life; your

partner has to have a life. If his or her social life is better than yours, create more activities in your life, so you do not feel left out and jealous.

16. Be supportive. You need to be your person's rock. You need to be the person he or she counts on, not the I-told-you-so pain in the ass. If your partner wants to start a band in the basement, don't shit on his or her ideas. Be supportive. Be nice.

17. Apologize. Make it count. If you are sorry about something, show total sincerity. Don't let it happen again and have to constantly be that fuckup who screws up everything all the time.

18. Forgive and live in the now. Don't hold a grudge. Don't bring up something from two years ago. *Let it go*!

19. Trust. Without trust, you just don't have much of a relationship at all. You either trust the person, or you don't. If you don't, you need to rethink being in the relationship.

20. Sacrifice. You may have to move to a suck-ass town to be supportive of your partner's growing career. You may have to give up the idea of

having another child. You may have to have the small piece of chicken at dinner. Sacrifice is *hard*. It never ends. You both have to be willing to do some sacrificing. This ain't easy.

Couple Goals Activity Sheet

1) Name something kind you will do for the other person every day.

   _____
   _____
   _____

2) Name two rituals you will do with each other every week (e.g., brunch every Sunday, Netflix every Wednesday, and so on).

   _____
   _____
   _____

3) Agreed-upon number of sex dates per week:

   _____

4) Agreed-upon division of financial obligations:

Theirs/Yours

$ Home Division:

_____

$ Utilities: _____

$ Automotive

_____

$ Food:

_____

$ Phone:

_____

$ Insurance:

_____

$ Car:

_____

$ Savings:

_____

$ Cable/Internet:

_____

$ Entertainment:

_____

$ Loans:

_____

$ Credit Cards:

_____

$ Other:

_____

5) Couples who play together stay together. List ten vacations or getaways you will take together in the next ten years:

1.

2.

3.

4.

5.

6.

7.

8.

9.

10.

6) Major purchases in the next five years:

_____

_____

_____

_____

7) Family planning in the next five years:

_____

_____

_____

_____

8) Where do you want to be in the next five to ten years in terms of family, finances, and career?

_____

_____

_____

_____

9) Where does your partner want to be in the next five to ten years in terms of family, finances, and career?

_____

_____

_____

_____

10)   Name something *you* will do for your partner to make his or her life happier.

_____

_____

_____

_____

11)   Name something he or she will do for you to make your life happier.

_____

_____

Chapter 9

The Wrap-Up

If you are *done* being a singleton, done being alone on Saturday night, then let this be a jump-start and a big kick in the butt to get you out there and help you take more control of your social life. Keep in mind that the more you get out of the house and meet people face-to-face, the better your odds are of finding your person. Take deliberate action today to make that happen.

Work on *you*. Get yourself together. The happier you are with yourself, the easier it is to be in a relationship with someone else. Put yourself out there now. There is no time like the present. Join that activities club, create an awesome online profile, and hit up your friends to make some introductions. Again, you are not desperate; you are assertive and proactive.

Keep your radar up for weirdos, frauds, and life-sucking assholes. If it feels off, it *is* off. Stay away from the red-flaggers of the world.

Please, know your triad. Know your lane. Be aware of it. If you don't like the lane you are in, make some changes and move out of it. Nothing is set in stone. You don't have to be Fatty Fatterson in the chub lane forever. You don't have to be Dicky Dickerwitz in the asshole lane until you die. Nor do you have to live in the HotMess O'Hara lane, scraping the bottom of the barrel for decades. Know thyself. Be strong. Make changes.

Also, hey! Be a good person. Be honest. Give people a chance, or just be courteous enough to let them know how you feel if you are not interested. Kindness is a lost art these days. On a side note, it's sad that I have to actually remind people not to be little bitches.

Crawl out from behind your phone, please. Make *real* connections with people. A four-word text is not a relationship. Talk, laugh, be present, and be responsive. Be curious.

And finally, when you have found a good one, the one who makes you laugh, who actually gives a shit about your well-being and likes you *just the way you are*, warts and all—the one you want to watch Netflix with and eat noodles with—don't fuck it up. Don't smother him or her. Don't take him or her for granted. Know you got a good one. Know that this is precious. Be aware when your golden goose (your person) has arrived, and hold on tight.

Made in the USA
Lexington, KY
27 March 2018